19□4
/Nine

. . . .

David Simpson & Richard Callag...

MYYEOr

MY
WOrLD
Designed by **courage**

Text copyright © David Simpson and Richard Callaghan
Design copyright © **courage**

ISBN: 978 1 901888 81 2

First Published 2013

Published in Great Britain by:
My World
Chase House
Rainton Bridge Business Park
Tyne and Wear
DH4 5RA
Tel: 0191 3055165

www.myworld.co.uk

My World is an imprint of Business Education Publishers Ltd.

British Cataloguing-in-Publications Data.
A catalogue record for this book is available from the British
Library.

Printed in Great Britain by Martins the Printers Ltd.

1964

/Nineteen Sixty Four

New Year's Day, **1964** saw Top of the Pops broadcast on British television for the first time. It ran on Thursday nights between 1964 and 1996, before it was moved to Friday night. The show featured performances by the week's top musical acts, as well as a chart run down. The first show featured The Rolling Stones with "I Wanna Be Your Man", Dusty Springfield with "I Only Want to Be With You", the Dave Clark Five with "Glad All Over", The Hollies with "Stay", The Swinging Blue Jeans with "Hippy Hippy Shake" and was closed by that week's number one single, the Beatles performing "I Want to Hold Your Hand".

The trial of the Great Train Robbers, one of the biggest of the decade, commenced in **January 1964**. It took place in the converted offices of a district council in Aylesbury, Buckinghamshire because the local courtroom was too small to accommodate all the lawyers and journalists. Thirteen defendants were held in a local prison and brought to trial every day. Although one of the number was acquitted, 12 were sentenced in **April 1964**. Seven of the men were sentenced to 30 years while four others received sentences of between 20 and 25 years. A solicitor who had failed to give vital information that would have led to their capture was sentenced to 3 years. The most dangerous of the gang, Charles Wilson, escaped from prison in **August 1964** and was recaptured in Canada in 1968. Another, Ronnie Biggs would escape in 1965 and evaded capture until 2001 when he voluntarily returned to Britain from Brazil.

EAST MEETS WEST IN JERUSALEM

In **January 1964**, Pope Paul VI began a three day visit to the cradle of Christianity in a tour which took in Jerusalem and Nazareth amidst tight security. On the second day an historic meeting took place in Jerusalem between the Pope and Patriarch Athenagoras, the leader of the Eastern Orthodox Church. The Eastern Orthodox Church had broken away from Rome almost 1,000 years previously and this was the first meeting of the leaders of the two churches in over 500 years.

1964 Number 1 Singles

The Beatles	/ I Want to Hold Your Hand / 10 December 1964
The Dave Clark Five	/ Glad All Over / 14 January 1964
The Searchers	/ Needles and Pins / 28 January 1964
The Bachelors	/ Diane / 18 February 1964
Cilla Black	/ Anyone Who Had a Heart / 25 January 1964
Billy J.Kramer and The Dakotas	/ Little Children / 17 March 1964
The Beatles	/ Can't Buy Me Love / 31 March 1964
Peter and Gordon	/ World Without Love / 21 April 1964
The Searchers	/ Don't Throw Your Love Away / 5 May 1964
The Four Pennies	/ Juliet / 19 May 1964
Cilla Black	/ You're My World / 26 May 1964
Roy Orbison	/ It's Over / 23 June 1964

On **January 18, 1964** the design for what became – for a time - the tallest building in the world, was unveiled to the public. The idea for a World Trade Centre was first suggested in 1943 and a site in New York was earmarked in 1961. American architect, Minoru Yamasaki (1912-1986) was selected for the task in 1962. Ironically, Yamasaki, a second generation Japanese American, had a fear of heights. Acquisition of the site began in 1965, followed by site clearance and commencement of the work in 1966. The topping out ceremony would not take place until December 1970 and the complex itself finally opened in April 1973. Yamasaki's iconic twin towers dominated New York's skyline until their destruction in the terrorist attack of September 11, 2001.

Nicholas Cage /
7 January 1964 / American movie star

Michelle Obama /
17 January 1964 / First Lady of the United States

Jane Horrocks /
18 January 1964 / English actress

Bridget Fonda /
27 January 1964 / American actress

Sarah Palin /
11 February 1964 / American politician, former Governor of Alaska

Chris Farley /
15 February 1964 / American comedian and actor (d. December 18, 1997)

Christopher Eccleston /
16 February 1964 / English actor, ninth Doctor

Bebeto /
16 February 1964 / Brazilian World Cup winning centre forward

Lee Evans /
25 February 1964 / British comedian and actor

Brett Easton Ellis /
7 March 1964 / American author, known for *The Rules of Attraction* and *American Psycho*

ZULU

Released on **January 22, 1964**, *Zulu* became one of the year's biggest cinematic hits. A dramatisation of the 1879 Battle of Rorke's Drift, *Zulu* starred Stanley Baker, Jack Hawkins, Ulla Jacobsson and Michael Caine, and was well received by critics and audiences alike. Director and producer Cy Endfield had been forced to leave his native United States after being placed on McCarthy's blacklist, settling in the United Kingdom where he co-wrote and co-produced *Zulu*. *Zulu* is widely regarded as one of the greatest British movies of all time, and spawned a 1979 prequel, *Zulu Dawn*.

DR STRANGELOVE

The **January 29** release of the comedy movie with the cumbersomely long title of *Dr Strangelove or: How I Learned to Stop Worrying and Love the Bomb* was one of the memorable movie moments of 1964. Directed, written and produced by Stanley Kubrick, the film featured Peter Sellers starring in three separate roles including the wheel-chair bound former Nazi nuclear nuclear weapons expert doctor of the title. The film follows a US President (also played by Sellers) who tries to recall a nuclear bombing mission ordered by a crazy US general (played by George C.Scott).

The first ticket collecting machines were installed on the London Underground in **1964**. It began with an installation at Stamford Brook station early in the year, followed by similar experimental installations at Chiswick Park and Ravenscourt Park. These ticket-reading machines were only present on the inward barriers and dealt with day travel tickets rather than season tickets which were handled by the usual manual barriers. Outward barrier ticket machines were not trialled on the Underground until May 1965.

The 36th
ACADEMY AWARDS

13th April, 1964 Presents...

Best Picture
Tom Jones

Best Director
Tony Richardson
Tom Jones

Best Actor
Sidney Poitier
Lilies of the Field

Best Actress
Patricia Neal
Hud

Best Supporting Actor
Melvyn Douglas
Hud

Best Supporting Actress
Margaret Rutherford
The VIPs

Conflict between the Turkish and Greek communities in Cyprus had resulted in the formation in **1964** of the United Nations Peacekeeping Force in Cyprus or UNFICYP. Fighting intensified in February 1964 in the port town of Limassol in which 21 people were killed. The UN Security Council passed Resolution 186 on March 4. The peace keeping force arrived later that month and continued to escalate into August when the UN negotiated a ceasefire.

BOOK BANNED

A novel published in 1748 fell victim to British censorship in **1964**. The pornographic novel *Fanny Hill* by John Clelland was first been banned back in 1749 but underground copies were distributed during the nineteenth century. In 1963 a British publisher called Mayflower Books, emboldened by the collapse of the 1960 obscenity trial regarding the publication of *Lady Chatterley's Lover*, published an unedited copy of the book. A police officer purchased a copy of the book after it was spotted in the window of a shop on London's Tottenham Court Road. A Bow Street magistrate granted a search warrant for the shop and 171 copies of the book were seized. Ralph Gold, owner of the bookshop, was put on trial in February 1964 and found guilty of breaking the obscenity laws.

Peter Sellers marries Britt Ekland

1964 saw Britt Ekland become a star overnight as she married actor and comedian Peter Sellers. Sellers had seen her photograph in a newspaper, and then proposed after meeting her in London. The whirlwind romance saw the couple marry on February 19 only 10 days after they had first met. Ekland and Sellars had a daughter, Victoria Sellers, in January 1965, and made three films together, *Carol for Another Christmas* (1964), *After The Fox* (1966) and *The Bobo* (1967), before divorcing in 1968.

On February 21, 1964 £10 bank notes were reintroduced in the UK. Production of all Bank of England bank notes of a value of £10 and above ceased during the Second World War for fear of mass Nazi forgery. In 1970, £20 notes would be reintroduced, followed by £50 notes in 1981.

On February 25, 1964, in Miami Beach, Cassius Clay became Heavyweight Champion of the World after defeating Sonny Liston. Liston retired before the seventh round, complaining of a shoulder injury, and the 22 year old from Louisville Kentucky became Champion of the World, claiming for himself the title which he would keep from then on, "The Greatest". The following day, Clay announced he was changing his name to Cassius X, and the following week he took on the name by which the world would know him, Muhammad Ali.

PRINCE EDWARD BORN

On **March 10, 1964**, Queen Elizabeth II gave birth to her fourth child, and third son, Edward Antony Richard Louis. At the time of his birth, Edward was third in line to the throne of ten Commonwealth nations, and was styled His Royal Highness The Prince Edward. He has since become Prince Edward, Earl of Wessex, taking the title on his 1999 marriage to Sophie Rhys-Jones.

Southampton becomes a city

1964 saw Southampton become the first new city of Queen Elizabeth II's reign, and the largest city in Hampshire. Southampton had originally applied for the granting of city status in 1958, but had been turned down. The charter granting city status, as well as the city's seal, came at a cost of

£72 13S 6D.

Taylor-Burton Wedding

1964 was the year that Holywood stars Richard Burton and Elizabeth Taylor were married for the first time. The couple met on the set of the movie Cleopatra in 1963 when they were both already married and the affair began. Once their respective divorces came through the couple were free to wed and on March 15, a Sunday, their marriage took place in Montreal. Taylor claimed the marriage would last forever. It lasted up until their divorce in 1974. They would, however, remarry again in 1975, only to re-divorce in 1976. Burton was thus the fifth of Taylor's seven husbands and the fifth and sixth of her eight marriages.

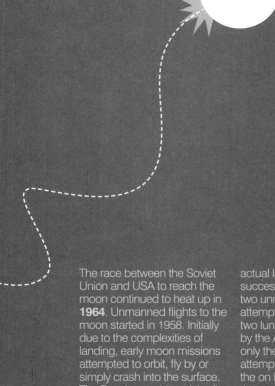

The race between the Soviet Union and USA to reach the moon continued to heat up in **1964**. Unmanned flights to the moon started in 1958. Initially due to the complexities of landing, early moon missions attempted to orbit, fly by or simply crash into the surface. The Russians achieved the first lunar impact in 1959 while the United States attempted three actual landings in 1962 without success. In 1964 there were two unmanned moon landing attempts by the Soviets and two lunar impact attempts by the Americans. Of these, only the American's second attempt was successful with the on board camera surviving the crash and returning 4,308 photos.

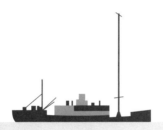

RADIO CAROLINE

On Easter Sunday, **1964**, Radio Caroline made its first broadcast from former Danish ferry Fredericia anchored three miles off the coast of Folkestone in Surrey, just outside British territory. Radio Caroline was one of the earliest pirate radio stations in Britain, flouting broadcasting rules from its position in international waters, and became famous as one of Britain's leading commercial radio stations.

First published in **1964**, Roald Dahl's *Charlie and the Chocolate Factory* would go on to be a true classic of children's literature. It is a book which has been delighting audiences young and old ever since, and has gone on to spawn two movie adaptations, 1971's *Willy Wonka and the Chocolate Factory*, starring Gene Wilder as Willy Wonka, and 2005's *Charlie and the Chocolate Factory*, with Johnny Depp taking on the role. Dahl wrote a sequel, *Charlie and the Great Glass Elevator*, in 1972, and had planned a third book, *Charlie in the White House*, although it was never completed.

Juliette Binoche /
9 March 1964 / French actress

Shane Richie /
11 March 1964 / English actor, singer and television personality

Rob Lowe /
17 March 1964 / American actor

David Cross /
4 April 1964 / American comedian and actor

Russell Crowe /
7 April 1964 / New Zealand born Australian actor, musician and film producer

Hank Azaria /
25 April 1964 / American actor, one of the chief voice actors on *The Simpsons*

John Parrott /
11 May 1964 / English snooker player

Lenny Kravitz /
26 May 1964 / American guitarist and singer

Kathy Burke /
13 June 1964 / English actress and comedian

Michael Laudrup /
15 June 1964 / Danish footballer and football manager

1964 saw the "British Invasion" really take hold in America, and no band was more responsible than The Beatles. This musical power shift was epitomised by the top 5 of the Billboard Hot 100 on **April 4, 1964**, when the top 5 singles in America were as follows:

The Beatles / "Can't Buy Me Love"

The Beatles / "Twist and Shout"

The Beatles / "She Loves You"

The Beatles / "I Want To Hold Your Hand"

The Beatles / "Please Please Me"

The award of an Oscar for best actor to Sidney Poitier at the Academy Awards on **April 13, 1964** was a major movie milestone. It was the first time that the coveted Best Actor award had been presented to a black actor. The Bahamian American actor received the award for his portrayal of Homer Smith in the 1963 film *Lilies of the Field*. Poitier had missed out on the award before, having been nominated for best actor (along with co-star Tony Curtis) in the 1958 film *The Defiant Ones*. Poitier wasn't the first black actor to receive an Oscar however. In 1963 James Baskett had received an honorary award for his 1948 performance as Uncle Remus in Walt Disney's *Song of the South* while Hattie McDaniel won the Best Supporting Actress Oscar for the 1939 film *Gone With The Wind*.

1964 saw the birth of a motoring icon as the first Ford Mustang rolled off the production lines. The car was introduced on **April 17, 1964,** and marked a stylistic shift in American cars, becoming the first of what became known as "Pony Cars". Originally, Ford had predicted they would sell under 100,000 cars in the first year, a target they beat within three months of the car's release. Indeed, another 318,000 Mustangs hit the road that year, and in the first 18 months Ford had produced more than a million of them. The Mustang has been in constant production ever since, inspiring many imitators, whilst always remaining a true American classic.

BBC

On **April 20, 1964**, Britain got a third television station as the BBC launched BBC 2. Initially only available in the London area, BBC 2 was envisaged as a place for more ambitious, less mainstream content than BBC1, its older counterpart. Broadcasting was supposed to begin on April 20, 1964, but following a fire at Battersea Power Station a huge power cut meant that it could not begin until 11 am the following day, with *Play School* the first programme to be officially shown on the channel.

7 UP

On **May 5, 1964** a remarkable documentary entitled *7 Up* was broadcast on ITV by Granada Television looking at the lives and expectations of fourteen seven year old British children from various social backgrounds. The programme was inspired by the motto "Give me a child until he is seven and I will give you the man". What made the programme particularly remarkable was its intention to update the viewers on the lives of the participants with follow-up documentaries every seven years. In the event next in the series entitled *14 Up* was broadcast in 1970 when the participants were 14-years of age. The eighth follow-up documentary *56 Up* was broadcast in May 2012 and featured all but one (ironically a TV documentary maker) of the original 14 participants.

1964 saw the first signs of public opposition to the Vietnam war amongst the American public, as twelve young men publicly burned their draft cards to protest the war. The protest occurred on May 12, in New York, and was the first of what would be many such protests against conscription and the war in Vietnam. The following year, an amendment to the law imposed harsh penalties for anyone who "knowingly destroys, knowingly mutilates" his draft card, as a direct response to this growing form of protest.

The year **1964** saw the conflict between the rival Mod and Rocker youth subcultures first begin to cause alarm and moral panic across the nation as the British press reported incidents of mass fights between the two opposing groups. It all seemed to kick off at Easter weekend on the beach at Clacton-on-Sea but on Whitsun weekend of May 18 and 19 the problem escalated with masses of Mods and Rockers heading to Margate, Broadstairs and Brighton to fight. The violence at Brighton spread along the coast to Hastings where it was dubbed the Second Battle of Hastings. The sensational way in which the press reported the events led to the sociologist Stanley Cohen developing the term "moral panic" in his 1970s study *Folk Devils and Moral Panics*.

At the 1964 Arab League Summit the Arab states set up a new organisation which intended to secure the liberation of Palestine. Chartered on **May 28, 1964** the Palestinian Liberation Organisation (PLO) called for the rights of Palestinian self-determination which it aimed to achieve through armed struggle. The PLO was headed by Ahmad Shukeiri until 1967 who was succeeded by Yahya Hammuda until February 1969 when the PLO's longest serving leader Yasser Arafat took command, remaining in the role until his death in 2004.

NELSON MANDELA
SENTENCED

June 12, 1964, saw Nelson Mandela, one of
the leaders of the African National Congress in
their struggle against Apartheid in South Africa,
sentenced to life imprisonment. The ANC's militant
wing, Umhkhonto we Sizwe (meaning "Spear of
the Nation") under Mandela's direction, had used
violence to fight against the oppressive Apartheid
regime. It was for his role in this campaign, as
well as for his wider position as a visible and vocal
opponent of the government, that Mandela was
sentenced to life in prison and transported to
Robben Island prison. Mandela would remain in
prison for almost three decades, his walk to freedom
in 1990 signalling the beginning of the end for the
Apartheid regime, and the rebirth of South Africa.

The Football League /
Liverpool won the league, their sixth title, with Manchester United finishing as runners up. A 17 year old from Belfast, George Best, made his debut for Manchester United this year

The FA Cup /
Won by West Ham United, beating Preston 3-2 to take the trophy for the first time. West Ham were 2-1 down with only minutes to go, scoring two in as many minutes to steal the glory

The Epsom Derby /
Won by Santa Claus, ridden by Scobie Breasley

The Grand National /
Willie Robinson rode Team Spirit to victory

Wimbledon Men's Singles Title /
Australian Roy Emerson defeated his compatriot Fred Stolle in the final

Wimbledon Ladies' Singles Title /
Brazilian Mario Bueno beat Australian Margaret Court to lift the title

The County Championship /
Worcestershire, with Warwickshire coming second

The Five Nations Championship /
Shared between Scotland and Wales, both finishing with 2 wins and 2 draws to their name

MONOKINI

The Austrian-American fashion designer Rudi Gernreich designed and launched the monokini in **1964**. Gernreich's swimwear was similar to a bikini but with the breasts bared and the briefs suspended from two straps in the cleavage that continued over the shoulders. The design proved popular with buyers but few were courageous enough to wear it in public. When girls at the Condor Club in North Beach San Francisco began wearing the monokini on June 22 it became the world's first topless bar. Some English designers were inspired by the idea and began designing topless evening wear. On August 21 three English women were arrested in London for wearing such dresses in public.

1964 saw one of, if not the greatest achievement of the Johnson administration, as the 1964 Civil Rights Act was signed into law on July 2. It outlawed discrimination against minorities, with particular attention paid to racial discrimination which had affected African Americans. It brought an end to racial segregation in schools, the workplace and in public, and addressed inequalities in voter registration. The bill had been called for by President John F. Kennedy in 1963, and following his death in the November it was left to President Lyndon Johnson to see the bill through Congress, passing the house with 289 votes for to 126 against, and the Senate 73 to 27.

At the height of Beatlemania, the four lads from Liverpool became more than just pop stars, they became movie stars with the release of their first film A *Hard Day's Night*. Released on July 6, written by Alun Owen, directed by Richard Lester, *A Hard Day's Night* was hugely well received both by audiences and critics, who lauded the performances both of the band and of the supporting cast. Owen's screenplay was nominated for an Academy Award, while the film took £2.5m at the box office from a budget of just £200,000.

An 89-year old Sir Winston Churchill made his last appearance in the House of Commons on **July 27, 1964**. The following day the Commons passed an all-party motion presented to Churchill at his London home near Hyde Park. It acknowledged Parliament's unbounded admiration for his services and remembered:

"above all, his inspiration of the British people when they stood alone, and his leadership until victory was won; and offers its grateful thanks to the Right Honourable Gentleman for these outstanding services to this House and to the nation."

Churchill continued to represent the constituency of Woodford as its MP right up until his retirement at the General Election on **October 15, 1964**.

On **August 13, 1964**, the last executions in Britain took place. Peter Anthony Allen was hanged at Walton Prison in Liverpool, whilst Gwynne Owen Evans was executed simultaneously, at Strangeways Prison in Manchester. Both men had been convicted of the same crime, the murder of John Alan West, a 53 year old van driver from Seaton in Cumberland. The passage of laws to abolish capital punishment the following year meant that these were the last times that the death penalty was carried out in the United Kingdom.

On **August 22, 1964**, at six thirty in the evening, the very first edition of Match of the Day was broadcast. That night it featured the highlights of just one match, Liverpool's 3-2 win over Arsenal at Anfield. BBC 2 was only available in London at the time, and only 20,000 people tuned in for that evening's programme, witnesses to the birth of an English football institution.

Courtney Cox /
15 June 1964 / American actress

Craig Charles /
11 July 1964 / English actor, Lister in *Red Dwarf*

Gaby Roslin /
12 July 1964 / English television presenter

Ross Kemp /
21 July 1964 / English actor and broadcaster

Barry Bonds /
24 July 1964 / American baseball player, 14 time All Star

Sandra Bullock /
26 July 1964 / American actress

Jurgen Klinsmann /
30 July 1964 / German football player and manager

Adam Yauch /
5 August 1964 / American rapper, The Beastie Boys' MCA (d. May 4, 2012)

Keanu Reeves /
2 September 1964 / Canadian actor

Janeane Garofalo /
28 September 1964 / American actress and comedian

August 27, 1964, saw the release of Disney's *Mary Poppins*, the Julie Andrews and Dick Van Dyke starring musical extravaganza which would go on to be one of the most enduring family movies of all time. Andrews, who had been passed over for the role of Eliza Doolittle in *My Fair Lady*, took home the Oscar for Best Actress for her performance, with the film picking up four more awards out of a total of 13 nominations. The story of a supernatural nanny in an Edwardian London home, *Mary Poppins* captivated audiences in 1964, and has continued to do so ever since, becoming one of Disney's most popular classics.

1964 Number 1 Singles

The Animals / House of the Rising Sun / 7 July 1964

The Rolling Stones / It's All Over Now / 14 July 1964

The Beatles / A Hard Day's Night / 21 July 1964

Manfred Mann / Do Wah Diddy Diddy / 11 August 1964

The Honeycombs / Have I The Right / 25 August 1964

The Kinks / You Really Got Me / 8 September 1964

Herman's Hermits / I'm Into Something Good
/ 22 September 1964

Roy Orbison / Oh Pretty Woman / 6 October 1964

Sandie Shaw / Always Something There To Remind Me
/ 20 October 1964

Roy Orbison / Oh Pretty Woman (again)
/ 10 November 1964

The Supremes / Baby Love / 17 November 1964

The Rolling Stones / Little Red Rooster / 8 December 1964

The Beatles / I Feel Fine / 8 December 1964

The Forth Road Bridge, which spans the Firth of Forth, connecting Edinburgh to Fife was opened by Queen Elizabeth II and the Duke of Edinburgh on September 4, 1964. The bridge itself is 8,241 feet long, and 108 feet wide, and replaced the ferry service which had existed, in some form or other, since the 11th century. At the time of the bridge's construction, it was the fourth longest suspension bridge in the world, and the longest outside the United States, and is made up of 39,000 tonnes of steel and 115,000 cubic metres of concrete.

THE Sun

First published on **September 15, 1964** as a broadsheet, The Sun was launched as a replacement for the failing Daily Herald, and retained the Herald's strong left wing bias. It was not until 1969 that it became a tabloid, after it had been purchased by Rupert Murdoch's News International. The Sun's initial circulation was around 3.5 million, but that had fallen by 1969, leading its owners to sell it to Murdoch, who overhauled the paper and turned it into one of Britain's best selling daily newspapers.

Harry Hill /
1 October 1964 / English comedian, author and television presenter

Clive Owen /
3 October 1964 / English actor

Yasmin Le Bon /
29 October 1964 / British Model

Marco van Basten /
31 October 1964 / Dutch football player, three time European Player of the Year, 1992 World Player of the Year

Famke Janssen /
5 November 1964 / Dutch actress, star of *Goldeneye* and the *X-Men* trilogy

Alistair McGowan /
24 November 1964 / English impressionist and actor

Don Cheadle /
29 November 1964 / American actor

Teri Hatcher /
8 December 1964 / American actress, star of *Desperate Housewives* and *Lois and Clark: The New Adventures of Superman*

Steve Austin /
18 December 1964 / American actor and former professional wrestler

Eddie Vedder /
23 December 1964 / American rock star, lead singer of Pearl Jam

GOLDFINGER

September 17, 1964 saw the release of the film many consider to be the classic Bond movie, Goldfinger. The third film to feature Sean Connery as the suave British secret agent, Goldfinger was also the first big budget Bond, costing as much to produce as the previous two combined. It was the first Bond movie to feature many of the tropes which have gone on to characterise the series, including the use of technology and gadgets, and a pre-credits action sequence. It was the first Bond to win an Academy Award, and was hugely commercially and critically successful, making back its $3 million budget in a fortnight. It went on to take $124.9 million at the box office, and cement its place in cinematic history.

INDEPENDENT MALTA

The island of Malta achieved independence from Britain on September 21 following negotiations with the United Kingdom headed by the Maltese Prime Minister Giorgio Borg Olivier. The Maltese people voted for independence in a constitutional referendum which was approved by more than 54 percent of the voters. From **1964** until 1974 Malta would be a constitutional monarchy with Elizabeth II as its head of state but it eventually became a Republic in 1974 appointing a president as its head of state, within the commonwealth.

COLD WAR AIRCRAFT

The first flight of a supersonic aircraft designed for Cold War combat took place on **September 27, 1964**. This high-speed aircraft called the TSR-2 was an expensive project intended to have a tactical role. It was designed to target high value targets in well-defended areas at low altitude with either nuclear or conventional weapons. It would also have an important role in capturing reconnaissance photos at high speed. A further 24 test flights took place with the last in March 1965 but the following month the project was controversially scrapped due to escalating costs.

1964 saw the birth of the computer programming language BASIC. The word is an acronym meaning Beginner's All-Purpose Symbolic Instruction Code. The original BASIC was known as Dartmouth BASIC from its birthplace, Dartmouth College in New Hampshire, USA where it was designed by John George Kemeny and Thomas Eugene Kurtz. It enabled non-science students to access to computers at a time when access to computers tended to be through writing custom software which tended to be the sole domain of mathematicians and scientists.

On **October 1, 1964**, the first of Japan's famous bullet trains made its way from Tokyo to Osaka, as the Tokaido Shinkansen line opened. Construction had started in 1959, and the opening coincided with the 1964 Tokyo Olympics, which started on October 10. The train that day reached 210 km/h, but since then the top speed has actually increased, to around 270 km/h today. Linking Tokyo, Nagoya and the Osaka-Kobe-Kyoto metropolitan area, the Tokaido Shinkansen is the most heavily travelled line in Japan, and one of the most heavily travelled in the world.

TOKYO ● 1964

The **1964** Tokyo Olympics, taking place between October 10 and October 24, saw a number of notable victories for Britain. Golds were seized in both the men's and women's long jump with successes for Mary Rand and Welshman Lynn Davies. Rand also scooped the silver in the Pentathlon. Ann Packer took the gold in the Women's 800 metres and the silver in the 400 metres. In the men's 20km walk Britain's Ken Matthews took gold. It seemed that for the first time the 100 metres was run under 10 seconds with an astonishing time of 9.9 seconds in the 100 metres semi-final by American Bob Hayes but the record was disallowed because of the wind. Hayes went on to win the gold equalling the world record with a time of 10 seconds. One of the big stars of the Olympics was American swimmer Don Schollander who took four gold medals including world record breaking swims in the 100 and 400 metre freestyle events.

1964 saw a major power shift in the Soviet Union, as Nikita Khruschev was forced from power and replaced as leader of the USSR by Leonid Brezhnev. Khruschev had been responsible for beginning the process of "de-Stalinisation" in the Soviet Union, as well as supporting the country's first forays into space, and had been at the helm when the Cold War came the closest to heating up, during the Cuban Missile Crisis. Khruschev was removed from power, the Presidium and Central Committee accepting his voluntary resignation on October 14. He was replaced by Brezhnev, who would spend 18 years as leader of the country, a tenure second only to that of Stalin.

UK General Election

October 15, 1964, saw Harold Wilson lead the Labour Party back to Downing Street for the first time for 13 years. Labour won 317 seats to the Alec Douglas-Home led Conservatives' 304, with the Liberals taking 9 seats to make up Parliament. Labour's slim 4 seat majority made Wilson unable to follow through on his party's pledge to nationalise the steel industry, and led to him calling another election in 1966 in the hope of increasing his grip on Parliament.

The People's Republic of China made its way onto the biggest stage of all in **1964**, with the country's first nuclear test. The test took place on October 16 at the Lop Nur test site in north western China, and had a yield of 22 kilotons. With the test, China became the world's fifth nuclear power, joining the United States, Soviet Union, United Kingdom and France. Mao Zedong had believed that China would only be taken seriously as a world power if it possessed a nuclear weapon, and the Lop Nur test marked the culmination of that ambition.

Zambia declared independence from the United Kingdom on **October 24, 1964**. Kenneth Kaunda, leader of the National Independence party and until then the country's Prime Minister, became the country's first President. Kaunda would be leader of Zambia until 1991.

On **October 29, 1964**, the Star of India, a 563 carat star sapphire believed to be one of the largest in the world, was stolen from the American Museum of Natural History in New York. Thieves unlocked a bathroom window during museum opening hours and used it to gain entry. Upon entering the museum they discovered that the Star of India was the only stone secured with an alarm, and the alarm's battery was dead so they took the Star, along with other gems including the de Long Ruby and the Eagle Diamond and fled. Within two days notorious cat burgler Jack Murphy was arrested, along with two accomplices, and later sentenced to three years in prison. The Star of India turned up months later in a locker at a Miami bus station.

A new soap made its debut on ITV in **November 2, 1964**. *Crossroads*, set in a Birmingham motel featured actress Noele Gordon as Meg Richardson, a wealthy woman who had converted her Georgian mansion using compensation money paid to her after a motorway was built through her land. The soap was not initially broadcast by all the independent regional television channels and Granada, producers of Coronation Street would not show *Crossroads* until the 1970s when it became a close rival of their popular soap.

Lyndon B. Johnson, who had assumed the presidency following the assassination of John F. Kennedy in 1963, was returned to the White House in a landslide on **November 3, 1964**, taking 61.1% of the popular vote, sweeping 44 states and the District of Columbia, and leaving his right wing Republican opponent Barry Goldwater trailing in his wake. It was a monumental victory for LBJ, ushering in the most liberal government in America since that of Franklin D. Roosevelt, and reducing the Republicans to the fringe of American politics. Unfortunately for Johnson, a combination of right wing reaction to his radical social agenda, and splits in his own party caused by the deepening conflict in Vietnam would restrict him to one full term in office, but in 1964 everything looked bright for the Democrats.

In **1964** Donald Campbell became the only person to set a land speed and water speed world record in the same year. On July 17 he set a land speed record of 403.1mph at the dried salt lake of Lake Eyre in South Australia in his Bluebird-Proteus CN7. It was not until the very end of the year that he would set a new water speed record too achieving a speed 276.33mph at Lake Dumbleyung, Western Australia on December 31 in his Bluebird K7.

3.276

BILLION

That's the number of people who lived in the world in 1964.

If you were around in 1964 apologies if we missed you out.

Just in case we did, here's the revised figure:

3.276 billion and **one** people lived in the world in 1964.